An Artist _____ _____ nomie

by J. L. Georgia
illustrated by Jane Wallace-Mitchell

Harcourt
SCHOOL PUBLISHERS

11 ©Penguin Young Readers Group, a member of Penguin Group (USA); 12, 14 ©Rob Cruse

Copyright © by Harcourt, Inc.

Printed in China

ISBN 10: 0-15-351435-3
ISBN 13: 978-0-15-351435-7

Ordering Options
ISBN 10: 0-15-351212-1 (Grade 2 Advanced Collection)
ISBN 13: 978-0-15-351212-4 (Grade 2 Advanced Collection)
ISBN 10: 0-15-358070-4 (package of 5)
ISBN 13: 978-0-15-358070-3 (package of 5)

4 5 6 7 8 9 10   985   15 14 13 12 11 10 09 08

An Artist Named Tanzie

Illustrated by Jane Wallace MacNeil

HARCOURT

In 1938, when Tomie dePaola was just four years old, he already knew what he wanted to do when he grew up. He told everyone his grand plans to write stories and draw illustrations for books.

When he was little, Tomie would sit on his Irish mother's knee and listen with interest to traditional stories from Ireland. She would read to him every day.

Besides his mother's stories, Tomie also loved the tall tales that his Irish grandfather told him. Tomie would later use traditional Irish stories and tall tales for some of his books.

Tomie loved listening to stories, but what he really wanted to do was to read himself. When he started kindergarten, he asked his teacher when he would be taught to read. She told him that he would not learn to read until first grade, which was the next year.

Tomie said he would come back next year. Then he walked out the door, down the stairs, and all the way home! He immediately picked up a book and tried to teach himself to read.

Of course, Tomie had to go back to school. He was thrilled when he started first grade, and he quickly learned to read. He had a huge appetite for stories, and he read everything he could find.

When he was about ten years old, Tomie received some art supplies as a present. He thought they were the best gift ever.

His parents gave him some room in the attic, and there Tomie would draw and draw. No one was allowed beyond the invisible line into his drawing place unless he invited them.

    At school, the art teacher noticed what
a good artist Tomie was. She would make
sure he got extra paper for his drawings.
Tomie would draw pictures for the children
in his class. He would create paper dolls
and give them to the girl who was his
favorite that week.

When Tomie grew up, he went to the same art school as his twin cousins. He remembered what his cousins told him. To be a good artist, he would need to practice, practice, practice! That's just what Tomie did.

When Tomie finished school, he became an art teacher. He got his first book job in 1965. It was illustrating a children's science book called *Sound Science*. Not long after that, he wrote and illustrated his first book.

People love Tomie's books. He has received many awards for literature—some for his illustrations and some for his stories. The first major award he received was the Caldecott Honor book award for his illustrations in *Strega Nona*.

Tomie dePaola achieved his dreams of becoming a writer and an illustrator. Today he continues to write and illustrate books that are enjoyed by people of many ages.

Tomie loves to write stories and illustrate books. He really likes it when children tell him how much they love his stories!

Think Critically

1. What caused Tomie to become interested in stories?

2. What gift did Tomie receive when he was ten years old?

3. Did you think Tomie would become a famous author and illustrator?

4. How can you tell that this book is not a story?

5. Would you like to read one of Tomie's books? Why or why not?

 **Social Studies**

Write a Biography Write a short biography telling about someone in your family. If possible, include photographs of the person, or draw a picture.

 **School-Home Connection** Tell a family member about the book. Then talk about what you would like to do when you grow up.

Word Count: 489